SIGNS IN SUCCESS

Profiles of Deaf Americans

by Ron Podmore

Butte Publications, Inc.
Hillsboro, Oregon, U.S.A.

SIGNS IN SUCCESS
Profiles of Deaf Americans

Editor: Ellen Todras
Cover: Anita Jones
Page Design: Anita Jones
Photos, with permission: the subjects
Author photo: Carroll's Photography, Centralia, Washington

Butte Publications, Inc.
P.O. Box 1328
Hillsboro, OR 97123-1328
U.S.A.

ISBN 1-884362-02-8
Printed in U.S.A.

TABLE OF CONTENTS

INTRODUCTION

These five short biographies are about deaf people who have been successful in a variety of fields. These people did not give up their dreams of what they wanted to do. The stories were written to provide interesting reading about deaf people while helping you improve your reading skills. There are exercises to do before and after each story to help build those skills.

Each biography starts with the person's name and his or her picture. After that is a list of "key words" that are found in the story. Work with your teacher to learn the new concept/sign you will use for each key word. Before starting each story, look at the key words in the Glossary, and work with your teacher to learn the new words and definitions.

After each biography, answer the questions to test your comprehension. If you do not know an answer, go back and read the story to find the answer.

Have fun reading and think about your own dreams!

I. KING JORDAN

"Deaf people can do anything, except hear."

I. KING JORDAN

KEY WORDS

<u>Directions:</u>

1) Identify the following words from the Glossary. Copy each word onto a piece of paper.

2) With your teacher, learn the new word or sign you will use for each word.

(A) Imagine

(B) Gallaudet University

(C) Navy

(D) Graduated

(E) Believed

(F) Protested

(G) Campus

(H) Hired

Imagine what it would be like to fly an airplane. Imagine what it would be like to dive under water.

Imagine what it would be like to be President of the United States.

Imagine.
Imagine.
Imagine.

One man did just that. He imagined. He imagined that one day he would be president of a university—a university for deaf students.

For over 124 years, this university never had a deaf president. In 1988, this man became the eighth president of Gallaudet University. What is important is that I. King Jordan is the first deaf president in the 124-year history of Gallaudet University.

His name is I. King Jordan. The letter "I" stands for "Irving." King Jordan is not really a king. He lives in Washington, D.C., and his job is at Gallaudet University.

His house is on the grounds at Gallaudet University and he walks to work. Imagine living 200 feet away from where you work!

King Jordan was born in 1943 in Glen Riddle. Glen Riddle is a small town in Pennsylvania. King Jordan was not always deaf. He grew up being able to hear. He also served in the United States Navy. He served for four years.

One day in 1965, while he was in the Navy, King was riding his motorcycle. While he was riding his motorcycle, something terrible happened that changed the rest of his life. He was hit by a car and was badly hurt. He was in the hospital for a long time because his head was injured. As a result of the accident, he became deaf.

In 1966, King Jordan went to Gallaudet University. He studied hard and got good grades. He graduated from Gallaudet and then went to another university. In 1973, he accepted a job teaching psychology at Gallaudet University. He enjoyed teaching very much, and his students really liked him. Later, he was put in charge of the psychology department at Gallaudet University. Still later, he became the head of the entire Arts and Sciences department at Gallaudet University. This is a very big department.

Gallaudet University is a school for deaf students. The teachers at Gallaudet University teach in sign language. For 124 years, Gallaudet University did not have a deaf president. In 1988, when it was time to choose a new president, the leaders of Gallaudet chose a hearing person. This made the deaf students sad. They believed they should have a deaf president. Later they got angry and protested. The students closed down Gallaudet University. They would not let people come onto the campus.

After seven days, the university officers changed their minds and hired a president who was deaf. They chose Dr. I. King Jordan to be their eighth president. The students were very happy. Deaf people across America were happy.

Today, Dr. Jordan works at Gallaudet University. He and his wife Linda have two children; a son named King III, and a daughter named Heidi. Dr. Jordan likes his job. When he is not working, he likes to be outside. He likes to canoe, run, and hike in the mountains.

Someday, you may also become president. Maybe you would like to become the President of the United States. Remember what Dr. Jordan said: "Deaf people can do anything, except hear!" With hard work and studying, you can become what you want. Just imagine!

EXERCISES

Directions:
1) Read each sentence.
2) Cover it and ask yourself, "What does it want?"
3) Answer the question using information from the story. Write on a separate piece of paper.

1. What does "I" in I. King Jordan stand for? Is Dr. Jordan really a king? Explain your answer.

2. King Jordan said, "Deaf people can do anything hearing people can, except hear." What things can you do that hearing people can do? List as many as you possibly can. What is the one thing that you may not be able to do?

3. What have you imagined before? Would you like to put that imagination into something you really can do? Write what you would like to do when you become older.

4. Where was I. King Jordan born? In what state?

5. Dr. Jordan was not always deaf. At one time he could hear. What happened in 1965 that changed him?

6. If you were hearing, and all of a sudden you became deaf, how would you feel?

7. Where is Gallaudet University located? Why did it not have a deaf president for over 124 years?

8. Why were the students at Gallaudet University angry? What did they do?

For each Key Word below, create a different
sentence than the one used in the story.

    a.   Imagine
    b.   Gallaudet University
    c.   Navy
    d.   Graduated
    e.   Believed
    f.   Protested
    g.   Campus
    h.   Hired

Directions:
Write a short paragraph that gives some information
about Dr. I. King Jordan. Be sure you tell me:

    Where and when he was born
    How he became deaf
    What his job is
    What he does when he is not working.

Directions:
Draw a picture of Dr. I. King Jordan at work. What do
you think he does while he is at Gallaudet University?

GREG HLIBOK

"Learn to make the best of what you have."

GREG HLIBOK

KEY WORDS

Directions:

1) Identify the following words from the Glossary. Copy each word onto a piece of paper.

2) With your teacher, learn the new word or sign you will use for each word.

(A) Organized

(B) Surprised

(C) Problem

(D) Patient

(E) Remembers

(F) Explored

(G) Leadership

Greg Hlibok was very excited. Soon he and many other students would find out who the next president of Gallaudet University would be. Greg was hoping for a deaf president. For over 124 years, Gallaudet University had not had a deaf president. Gallaudet University is for deaf students. Why not have a deaf president?

When Greg found out that there would not be a deaf president, he became very sad. Then he became very angry. He decided that it was time for a deaf president. Within a few hours, he contacted many students. They were also angry. The students organized a protest. Every day, for one week, the students protested for a deaf president.

Greg led the students in their protest for a deaf president. He and the students were very successful! Newspapers and television cameras came to Gallaudet University. They wanted to record the news. Greg made sure the students were informed.

Greg made sure the message was heard. Many people learned about what was happening at Gallaudet University. A new name was created for this event. It was called the "Deaf President Now" movement. A man wrote a book called *The Week the World Heard Gallaudet about the Deaf President Now movement*. Many people from different countries heard about the protest.

Greg was surprised by all the attention from the newspapers and television stations. Greg did what he believed in. So did a lot of the other students. These students also believed in Greg. Greg knew what he wanted ever since he was a little boy.

Greg was born deaf. His parents are also deaf. So are his sister and two older brothers. But the rest of his family are all hearing. Communication is not a problem because they all sign.

Greg was always one who stood up for what he believed in. At age five he was placed in a hearing school. His parents thought he would learn a lot at that school. But Greg did not like it there. He was mad and he got into fights with other kids. Many other kids did not like Greg's "funny looking hearing-aids" on his chest.

The teacher often punished Greg but not the other kids.

8

The teacher talked with the other kids and listened to them, but not to Greg. So Greg told his parents he wanted to go to Lexington School for the Deaf. His parents wanted him to stay. They told him to be patient. Greg became stubborn. He said, "No!" He stopped signing to his parents! Soon his parents understood that he really wanted to go to Lexington School for the Deaf, and they agreed to let him go there. After that, Greg was very happy.

Greg had a lot of fun with his family when he was a child. He did a lot of traveling with them. He went to camp every summer. He was very creative at doing many things at camp.

Greg remembers one summer when his family traveled to Maine. They went to a National Park called Acadia. They stayed there for one month.

Only the ocean and forest were there, at Acadia. There was no television. Greg was bored at first. But later, he learned to "make the best of what he had." He became interested in nature. He learned to keep busy by exploring the forest. He also explored the beach. He really enjoyed staying at Bar Harbor. Greg was sad when he had to go back home. Soon summer ended and school started.

Ever since Greg was a little boy, he wanted to go to Gallaudet University. His mom went to school there. So did his brother. When Greg graduated from Lexington School for the Deaf, he decided to follow his brother and mom, and go to Gallaudet University. So he traveled to Washington, D.C. Greg knew many students who were already at Gallaudet University. He had made many friends at youth leadership camps.

Greg became involved in leadership activities at

Gallaudet University. He went to school and took many different classes. During his last year at Gallaudet University, he decided he wanted to become a lawyer. Today, Greg lives in New York City. He is studying to become a lawyer. He wants to be able to work with deaf people. He believes he can help with deaf rights.

Remember the protests at Gallaudet University? With Greg's leadership, the students succeeded. They forced a hearing president to leave. Soon another president came in. That man was Dr. I. King Jordan, and he was deaf. After 124 years of being a college for the deaf, something new happened. Deaf people finally got a deaf president for a deaf university!

EXERCISES

Directions:
1) Read each sentence.
2) Cover it and ask yourself, "What does it want?"
3) Answer the question using information from the
story. Write on a separate piece of paper.

1. Why did Greg get into fights with other students at
school?

2. Why did Greg stop signing to his family?

3. What kind of school did his parents send him to
first? Then where did they send him to school?

4. Did Greg have any problems signing with his family? Why or why not?

5. Why was Greg bored at first when he went to Bar
Harbor, Maine? What does it mean to "make the best
of what he had?"

6. What did Greg do to "make the best of what he
had"? Where did he go?

7. Why did Greg follow his brother and mother?
Where did Greg go?

8. How did he become active in school at Gallaudet
University?

9. How could you become active at your school?

<u>Directions:</u>
For each Key Word below, create a different
sentence than the one used in the story.

    a.   Organized
    b.   Surprised
    c.   Problem
    d.   Patient
    e.   Remembers
    f.   Explored
    g.   Leadership

<u>Directions:</u>
1) Explain what you would do to become more
involved with your school. How would you get your
friends to join you? How would you get new people
to join your activities?

2) Put your ideas on a large piece of construction
paper and share them with your class. List and explain
how you would/will become more involved in your
school.

MARY LOU NOVITSKY

"Hello, and welcome to Deaf Mosaic."

MARY LOU NOVITSKY

KEY WORDS
<u>Directions:</u>
1) Identify the following words from the Glossary. Copy each word onto a piece of paper.

2) With your teacher, learn the new word or sign you will use for each word.

(A) Participated

(B) Flood

(C) Victims

(D) Realized

(E) Determined

(F) Editor

(G) Emmy Award

(H) Struggle

(I) Married

Mary Lou Novitsky was born deaf in Johnstown, a small town in Pennsylvania. Her parents were deaf but her sister was hearing. When she was very young, her family moved to Ohio. There, Mary Lou went to the Alexander Graham Bell School. Then, when she was seven years old, her family moved back to Pennsylvania.

Mary Lou went to the Western Pennsylvania School for the Deaf in Pittsburgh, Pennsylvania.

While she was in school, she was involved with sports and other class activities. She graduated from school in 1974. Then she went to Gallaudet University.

In 1977, while a student at Gallaudet, Mary Lou participated in the Miss Deaf Pennsylvania contest. That same year, a terrible flood wiped out a large part of her home town. Her family were victims of the Johnstown Flood.

While Mary Lou attended Gallaudet University, she was involved with the student body government. She was the vice-president and student media director. Mary Lou participated in many events related to television. She "covered" the student body election, "The Newlywed Game," and "The Dating Game." Mary Lou soon realized what she wanted to do with her life. She wanted to work in television.

Mary Lou wanted to become involved with television, but many friends and family members said that was not possible. They said this to Mary Lou because she was deaf. Her family and friends felt it was impossible, a deaf person in television. Mary Lou continued because she believed in herself. She was determined.

As a student at Gallaudet University, there were no classes in television for people to take. So Mary Lou decided to study psychology and communications. She graduated from Gallaudet University in 1979 and got a job. Her first job after she graduated was at the National Captioning Institute (NCI).

Captioning was very new in 1979. Only a few television shows were captioned. Today, many television shows are captioned. After Mary Lou left NCI, she was hired at Gallaudet University full time. Her new job was as a production specialist. She worked as an editor and camera operator for campus television projects.

In 1985, a new program called "Deaf Mosaic" was created. "Deaf Mosaic" is a news magazine show about deaf people in America. For the first three years, Mary Lou worked "behind the camera" with Gil Eastman. She enjoys working both on and behind the set with Gil. Later, she became a producer and helped to educate both deaf and hearing people about deaf people.

Today, "Deaf Mosaic" reaches over 60 million homes. Ms. Novitsky is a five-time Emmy Award winner for her work as a co- producer/co-host of "Deaf Mosaic." The Emmy award is given to people every year for achievement in television.

Mary Lou has some advice she would like to give to deaf children. She wants all of you to:

1. Enjoy your life
2. Explore and experience the world around you
3. Overcome the struggle of being deaf
4. Think positive
5. Stay with your goal.

Mary Lou Novitsky continues to work with "Deaf Mosaic." She is married to Jerry Mabashov. They have two sons. Her first son, Mike, is three years old, and her second son, Dan, is a toddler. She and her family live in Crofton, Maryland, a small town outside Washington, D.C.

EXERCISES

Directions:
1) Read each sentence.
2) Cover it and ask yourself, "What does it want?"
3) Answer the question using information from the story. Write on a separate piece of paper.

1. Mary Lou Novitsky was born in Pennsylvania. Find a map of the United States and locate Pennsylvania. What are the major cities in Pennsylvania? What is the capital?

2. How old was Mary Lou when she and her family moved back to Pennsylvania?

3. What is a flood? Where is Johnstown, Pennsylvania? What happened in 1977 in Johnstown?

4. Does your state have a School for the Deaf? If there is a school for the deaf, what is its name? Where is it located?

5. In 1977, Mary Lou participated in the Miss Deaf Pennsylvania contest. This event helps young deaf women take pride in being deaf and deciding what their life goals are. What are some of the positive things you can think of about being deaf? Be specific.

6. When Mary Lou went to school at Gallaudet University, she became involved in student government, student activities, and television. What are some things that you are involved with at your school?

7. At first Mary Lou was advised not to become involved with television. Who gave her this advice?

18

8. Why did Mary Lou's family feel it was impossible for her to become involved with television?

9. What is the show "Deaf Mosaic"?

10. Today, deaf people can be involved with television. Would you like to be involved with television? Why or why not?

Directions:
For each Key Word below, create a different sentence than the one used in the story.

- a. Participated
- b. Flood
- c. Victims
- d. Realized
- e. Determined
- f. Editor
- g. Emmy Award
- h. Struggle
- i. Married

Directions:
Draw a picture that shows what you know about the words "victim" and "flood."

Directions:
Write a brief paragraph that gives some information about Mary Lou Novitsky. Be sure you tell me:

Where she was born
When she was born
What she did while at Gallaudet University
What she does at work with "Deaf Mosaic."

PHILIP BRAVIN

"Yes, you can!"

PHILIP BRAVIN

KEY WORDS
<u>Directions:</u>
1) Identify the following words from the Glossary. Copy each word onto a piece of paper.

2) With your teacher, learn the new word or sign you will use for each word.

(A) Residential

(B) Lexington School for the Deaf

(C) International

(D) Company

(E) Decisions

(F) Retired

(G) Provides

New York City is one of the largest, most exciting cities in the world. More than seven million people live there. People say that every person in New York City has a story to tell about his or her life. Our story begins in 1945, when Philip Bravin was born in New York City. Who is Philip Bravin? Well, read on and find out who he is!

Philip Bravin was born deaf. His parents and other people in his family are deaf also. His wife and children, some cousins, and other relatives are deaf. Philip had no problem learning how to sign when he was very

21

young. His parents taught him how to sign as soon as they could.

At the very young age of three, young Philip was sent to a residential deaf school. This school was in a neighborhood of New York City called Manhattan. The school was called the Lexington School for the Deaf. After 1968, it moved to Jackson Heights. Lexington used to be an "oral school." This means that deaf and hard-of-hearing students are taught some speech also. Young Philip communicated in sign language with his parents. But his parents thought it was important to learn how to speak, too.

From 1953 to 1961, Philip attended the New York School for the Deaf in White Plains, New York. In 1961, Philip graduated from the New York School for the Deaf. He then attended college at Gallaudet University, in Washington, D.C. In 1966, Philip graduated from Gallaudet University.

In 1968, Philip began work at a company called IBM. The letters "IBM" stand for International Business Machines. IBM is a very large company. IBM makes computers. These computers are sent all around the world. Philip enjoyed working at IBM for many years. In 1993, Philip retired from work at IBM. He had worked there for 25 years.

In 1982, Mr. Bravin became a member of the Board of Trustees at Gallaudet University. A trustee helps the president of the university make important decisions. Mr. Bravin became Chairman of the Board in 1988. In 1993, Philip retired from work at IBM. He had worked there for 24 years.

Today, Mr. Bravin keeps very busy. He is very active with many different jobs. He recently started his own company called "Yes, You Can!" This company provides marketing and services for deaf programs and deaf schools. Mr. Bravin is the new president for the National Captioning Institute (NCI) in Virginia. NCI helps to create words that appear on the television screen so that many deaf people can read them. Mr. Bravin likes his work and believes that "Yes, you can!"

EXERCISES

Directions:
1) Read each sentence.
2) Cover it and ask yourself, "What does it want?"
3) Answer the question using information from the story. Write on a separate piece of paper.

1. Who is Philip Bravin? What is unusual about his family?

2. Was Mr. Bravin born hearing or deaf? When did he start learning sign language?

3. What is meant about everyone in New York having a story to tell?

4. Where is the Lexington School for the Deaf? What kind of school is it?

5. In 1968, Mr. Bravin began working at IBM. What does "IBM" mean? What does this company make?

6. What is a "trustee" at Gallaudet University? How does a trustee help the president at a university?

7. What does it mean to retire? Do you know someone who is retired? Who?

8. What is a company? Mr. Bravin started his own company called "Yes, You Can!" What kind of work does "Yes, You Can!" do?

9. Do you know some companies in your town? List three of them and write about what they do. Do you know someone who works in a company? Who?

Directions:
For each Key Word below, create a different
sentence than the one used in the story.

<blockquote>

a. Residential
b. Lexington School for the Deaf
c. International
d. Company
e. Decisions
f. Retired
g. Provides

</blockquote>

Directions:
1) With your teacher, create your own company. Draw
a picture of what your company looks like.

2) Write a short paragraph that answers the following
questions:

<blockquote>

What does your company make?
Why did you choose this kind of work?
How will you get people to buy what you
make?

</blockquote>

MARLEE MATLIN

"It is important to follow your dreams, whatever they are.
If you believe in yourself, and work hard, you can reach
any goal you can imagine!"

MARLEE MATLIN

KEY WORDS

<u>Directions:</u>
1) Identify the following words from the Glossary.
Copy each word onto a piece of paper.

2) With your teacher, learn the new word or sign you
will use for each word.

(A) Mainstream

(B) Involved

(C) Academy Award

(D) Performing

(E) Doubts

(F) Continues

(G) Charities

(H) Closed Captioning

Have you ever had a dream? What was in your
dream? Have you ever wanted something so much, you
would not give it up? That is what Marlee did. She
would not give up.

Marlee Matlin was born and raised in Morton Grove,
Illinois. When she was 1 1/2 years old she became very
sick. She got the measles. When she became better, she
had lost most of her hearing.

When she was young, Marlee went to a public school

27

in Chicago with a mainstream program. "Mainstream" means that there were many hearing students with Marlee. Not all of the students were deaf. She had many friends who could hear. Many of her friends knew how to sign.

Marlee enjoyed school and had a lot of fun. If Marlee could return to school, she would do two things: First, she would become more involved with school activities. Second, she would not miss one day of school. Marlee remembers wearing a hearing aid when she was in school. Today, she wears one hearing-aid because it is helpful for her.

All her life, Marlee wanted to be an actress. When she was seven years old, she got her first role—as Dorothy in The Wizard of Oz. Marlee has appeared in many movies. She also has appeared on "*Sesame Street.*"

In 1987, Marlee got a very special award. This award was called the Academy Award. This award is given to actors and actresses who are very good at acting. Marlee got this award for a movie she acted in. It was called *Children of a Lesser God.* This movie was about life at a residential school for the deaf. Marlee was the first deaf person to receive the Academy Award. At age 21, she was also the youngest person at that time to receive the Academy Award for Best Actress.

Some of the other movies Marlee has starred in were *The Man in the Golden Mask, The Player,* and *The Linguini Incident.* She enjoyed performing in these movies. Acting is very hard work, but she enjoys watching the movie when it is finished. Her most recent movie is called *Hear No Evil.* The movie was filmed in Portland, Oregon. Marlee enjoyed the Pacific Northwest very much and spent some time visiting with deaf students there.

Marlee also starred in a TV series called *"Reasonable Doubts."* She continues to perform in many movies and TV shows. When Marlee is not acting, she likes to spend time with her friends and family.

Marlee has also received many awards for the work she does to help others. She is very involved with charities that help children and adults. One thing that is very important to her is closed captioning. Closed captioning means that the words that people say on television appear on the screen. The deaf and hard-of-hearing read these words and understand what the people on TV are saying. Marlee hopes that one day every TV show and video that people watch will be closed captioned. She would like everyone to be entertained and informed.

Marlee lives in Los Angeles with her husband, where she continues to follow her dreams and pursue her acting career. She would like you to remember one thing:

"Believe in yourself. Go after your dreams. They can come true!"

EXERCISES

Directions:
1) Read each sentence.
2) Cover it and ask yourself, "What does it want?"
3) Answer the question using information from the story. Write on a separate piece of paper.

1. Who is Marlee Matlin? What makes Marlee Matlin different from many other actresses?

2. Where did Marlee live when she went to public school? Where does Marlee live now?

3. "If you believe in yourself, and work hard, you can reach any goal you can imagine!" What do you think Marlee means by that?

4. Was Marlee born deaf or hearing? How do you know?

5. What does it mean to "act"? Have you ever acted? How?

6. How old was Marlee when she got her first acting role? What role did she play?

7. In 1987, Marlee received a very special award. What was it called? What was the story about in the movie that she acted in? List some other movies that Marlee has been in.

8. When Marlee is not acting, what does she like to do?

9. What does closed captioning mean? Why is closed captioning important to Marlee? Is it important to you? Why?

<u>Directions:</u>
For each Key Word below, create a different
sentence than the one used in the story.

    a.   Mainstream
    b.   Involved
    c.   Academy Award
    d.   Performing
    e.   Doubts
    f.   Continues
    g.   Charities
    h.   Closed Captioning

<u>Directions:</u>
1) Find a newspaper with a TV guide section.
2) Count how many TV shows have a closed caption
symbol (CC).
3) Compare three days of TV shows that have closed
captioning. For each day, plot the number of shows with
closed captioning on the graph below.

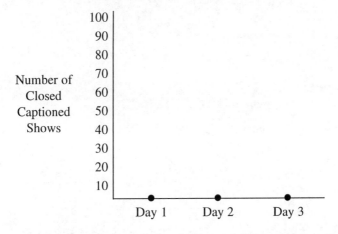

a. Which day had the most closed captioned shows?
b. Which day had the least closed captioned shows?
c. Would you watch TV shows just because they had
closed captioning? Why or why not?

Directions:
1. If you could be an actor, what would you want to be?

2. Write a story that begins with this title: "If I Could Be an Actor...."

3. Be sure to include the following:

> What kind of person or animal you would like to act as?
> What kind of story it is (For example, is it in a city, on a rocket ship, underwater? Where?)
> Who would be acting with you, and why you would choose that person.

GLOSSARY

Academy Award
award given to very good actors and actresses
Marlee Matlin won an Academy Award in 1987.

activity
being active; movement; use of power
Today's activity will be shooting basketballs.

angry
mad at someone or somebody
My mom was angry after I broke the window.

appear
to come into sight
The moon does not appear every night.

attend
to be present at
I must attend school today.

believed
thought something was true or real
My mother believed me when I told her the truth.

Board of Trustees
group of people who help a university president make decisions
The Board of Trustees met this morning.

bored
nothing to do or play with
My friends are gone; now I'm bored.

born
brought forth, natural birth
I was born on December 12, 1976.

camp
live away from home for a time in a tent or outdoors
I'm going to a sign language camp this summer.

campus
land that a university is on
I like to walk around the campus.

change
make different; become different
I need to change my wet clothes.

charities
giving money to help people who are poor; donations
We gave money to many charities at Christmas.

closed captioning
for deaf or hard-of-hearing: subtitles or words show
up on bottom of TV screen so disabled people can
comprehend
The movie had closed captioning.

company
group of people working for the same business
I got shoes from the Nike Company.

computer
machine to process information
I played word munchers on the computer.

continues
keeps on doing something
The teacher continues writing on the board.

cousin
family member: the child of an aunt or uncle
My cousin is coming for Christmas.

create
to make or invent something
I will create a checkerboard in wood shop.

"Deaf President Now" movement
This event in March 1988 at Gallaudet University resulted in its first deaf president.

decisions
making up one's mind to do things; judgments
Are you ever sorry about decisions you have made?

determined
having your own ideas, and not being swayed by others
She was determined to go to the university.

different
not alike; not like
That country is different from ours.

disabled
deprived of ability to do normal things in society
The man in the wheelchair is disabled.

doubts
not believing in some things
Sometimes I have doubts about his truthfulness.

dream
brain waves of the unconscious mind; pictures and images when asleep
I dream of food every night.

editor
person who decides what will be in a television project
The editor gave other people many directions.

Emmy Award
award given to people who have done good work in
television
She won an Emmy Award two years in a row.

entertain
interest; make fun for; amuse
The movie entertained us for two hours.

except
leaving out; other than
He ate all of the cookies, except one.

exploring
traveling over unknown land or seas for a purpose
I went exploring in my backyard.

fight
two or more people trying to hurt each other
I got in a fight with Tommy after school.

film
movie; motion picture
Marlee Matlin stars in the film *Children of a Lesser
God.*

flood
water covering what is usually dry land
Many homes were ruined in the flood.

follow
to be behind something's lead; to watch closely
I followed Tim to the store.

force
(1) power; (2) to control or try to control
Luke, may the force be with you.

Gallaudet University
university for the deaf in Washington, D.C.
The students went to Gallaudet University to learn.

goal
something you strive for
My goal is to play sports.

graduated
finished the courses at a school
My brother and sisters graduated from high school.

hired
paid someone to work
My neighbor hired me to walk her dog.

hospital
place where a hurt person goes for help
I got hit in the head with a rock, and I had to go to the hospital.

imagine
form a picture in the mind
I can imagine being rich.

international
between or among nations or countries
The countries made peace, according to international law.

involved
took part in; included
My aunt is involved in her acting classes.

king
a man who rules a country and its people
In America we don't have a king, we have a President.

37

leadership
ability to show the way to others
You show leadership when you set a good example.

Lexington School for the Deaf
school for the deaf in New York state
I will go to the Lexington School for the Deaf.

mainstream
school where deaf or hard-of-hearing students are in the
same classrooms as hearing students
My friend was in a mainstream classroom for three
years.

married
man and woman joined together as husband and wife
My parents got married 15 years ago.

Navy
America's armed service that is in charge of ships
My grandfather fought in the Navy in World War II.

New York City
city on the East Coast of the United States; largest city in
the U.S.A.
There are a lot of people in New York City.

New York School for the Deaf
school for the deaf in New York state
My cousin went to the New York School for the
Deaf.

organized
got together and put into working order
We organized a birthday party for our teacher.

participated
took part in activities
I participated in many activities at camp.

patient
going calmly through something that is not fun
I was patient and waited quietly.

performing
acting in public
Marlee likes performing in movies.

president
chief officer of a company, university, or club
Gallaudet University finally has a deaf president.

problem
matter of difficulty
The math problem was hard.

protested
formed a group saying they didn't like or want
something
The "Deaf President Now" movement was a protest.

provides
gives; supplies
The school provides pencils and paper.

psychology
study of the mind
I will study psychology.

punished
caused pain to someone for his or her actions
I was punished for breaking the window.

realized
understood clearly
I realized he was joking.

receive
to get something handed to you
When will I receive my paycheck?

relatives
members of a family
I have many relatives.

remembers
calls to mind again
She remembers when she was a baby.

residential
school where students live, too
There are many residential schools for the deaf.

retired
after working for a long time, you get paid to quit; to stop
working
My mother retired from work last year.

school
place of educational services
I go to school to learn.

stay
to remain somewhere
I will stay at the party until 12:00.

struggle
hard work or great effort
It was a struggle to get my homework done.

student
person in a school
I am a student at Jones High School.

successful
having success; having reached a goal
I want to be successful in school.

surprised
not expecting something, and it happened
I was surprised when my grades were so good.

television camera
machine that shows what will be recorded for
television show
The television camera was focused right on me.

terrible
something bad
The food tasted terrible.

victims
people who were injured from something that
happened
The victims of the plane crash were crying.

visit
go to see; come to see
I will visit you on Christmas.

Washington, D.C.
capital city of the United States
Would you like to visit Washington, D.C.?

world
the earth
To sail around the world is a great thing to.